The Essence of Nature

The Essence of Nature

Roger Homer

Copyright © 2024 Roger Homer

The moral right of the author has been asserted.

Apart from any fair dealing for the purposes of research or private study, or criticism or review, as permitted under the Copyright, Designs and Patents Act 1988, this publication may only be reproduced, stored or transmitted, in any form or by any means, with the prior permission in writing of the publishers, or in the case of reprographic reproduction in accordance with the terms of licences issued by the Copyright Licensing Agency. Enquiries concerning reproduction outside those terms should be sent to the publishers.

Troubador Publishing Ltd
Unit E2 Airfield Business Park
Harrison Road, Market Harborough
Leicestershire LE16 7UL
Tel: 0116 279 2299
Email: books@troubador.co.uk
Web: www.troubador.co.uk

ISBN 978 1 80514 506 6

British Library Cataloguing in Publication Data.
A catalogue record for this book is available from the British Library.

Printed and bound in Great Britain by 4edge Limited
Typeset in 11pt Minion Pro by Troubador Publishing Ltd, Leicester, UK

ABOUT THE AUTHOR

After graduating from London University, Roger Homer worked as a journalist, finally as a sub editor for the Sunday Express and Daily Mail, and for BBC TV News.

Later he qualified as a Licentiate of the National Council of Psychotherapists, working in private practice and for the Employment Service.

He aims to follow this first collection with three more, a play and a novel.

His interests include the Arts, psychology, philosophy, nature and the countryside and several sports.

He lives in Exmouth.

www.homerite.art/

Contents

Cityscapes

Rain rhythms	3
Play seen darkly	6
Behind the veil	7
The veil lifted	8
The old Black Country	9
Potteries afternoon 1966	11
Killer castle	13
London Pride	14
Guest house	15
Garden Suburb	16
South from Waterloo	18

Land & Sea

Seascapes	21
Sky pageant	23
November leaves	24
60s country station	25
Country station view	26
Echoes of the mill	27
Pictures of Cannock Chase	28
Virgin land	30
Ghosts of the quays	31
Town v Country	33

Creatures

Avian charmers	37
Vietcong	41
Butterflies	42
The Reverend Bug	43
Joybringer	44

People

Bike boys	47
Men of clay	49
Breadless in Battersea	51
Small-town	53
L.A. girls	54
Hospital days	55
Leaving hospital	59
The other side	60
Nemesis	61
Coach company	62
Bach-ing mad	64
Ode to Sibelius	65
The harpist	67
Sailors and others	68
Soul of Sidmouth	70

Preface

I must start with two definitions. The "Nature" in my title is used in the usual sense, but includes people. The "Essence" is my own view of its qualities.

When growing up I was constantly frustrated by demands to adapt to social values which clashed with my internal ones and had no *personal meaning*.

I soon learned that this feeling was shared by others. In fact, parents often marvelled at the aptness of their children's insights, expressed in language they'd never have thought of themselves.

Studying psychology helped explain this, as follows:

- From an upbringing of love, security and nurture of their selves, children's *values* take hold and grow. Confidence in the world around enables their expression in play.
- It is crucial here that *rate of adaptation* to society fits the *child's readiness* to absorb it.
- But I believe that today, pressure is increasing on children to adapt to the world we live in, while individual character and values are being lost.

So in these poems I have tried to recapture the "naive" approach and sharply focus on the essence of natural objects. I will be happy if my readers profit from the result.

R.H.

Cityscapes

Rain rhythms

I

Overhead a livid eiderdown, folds gathered,
is compressing light and air;

surely... those children outside
were playing happily:
now sound like souls long left behind.

Then I jump –
something crashing through jungle –

No: it's only rain,
thrashing down vertical,
rapping on leaves,
spitting from the ground
like angry fat from a pan.

Drumming blurs to a swish,
traffic creeps in a mist
through sudden-emptied streets,
people herding to shelter.

Faces crowd to windows
gripped by a nervous thrill
from something ... beyond.

II

City rain
somewhere in the sodden air,
in the sky of yellow-grey
blank and flat as plasterboard, but...

Ah, *there*!
Against the dark trunks of trees,
needles softly flitting.

Globule necklaces cling,
amplify, then fall;

the drops that drip keep coming on.

Puddles now! Who saw them form?
Down on the watery canvas
sky, trees and terraces are merging

and drops that drip keep coming on.

On rooftops
sunken clumps of feathers sit it out,
a thrush's song is tumbling defiance

but drops that drip keep coming on.

People brush off this rain,
its power to lull the mind,
conjuring images to expand reality;
and through the long and gloomy afternoon

the drops that drip keep coming on.

III

Night rain at wind's whim,
rolling regal across the sky,
hunting down in seething billows,
bucks, plunges, mane-tossing,
all drunk with freedom

then melts to mist,
hangs, coils, writhes,
wringing heart for its heart-ease.

Picks at windows,
scampers over,
oddly comforting ...

Then, shattering on glass, brain,
jolting you from armchair thoughts,
comes thicker, faster,
lashing house facades
till ripped away, it tears off,
swept against the racing moon.

Play seen darkly

My local theatre
in the round;
the black curtain edges back
on a silent ad-lib show.

Clouds banking, breaking up;
a chicken is chasing
a drooping dinosaur,
then changing
into a slice of Emmenthal.

But I struggle to name characters,
follow the plot and the action,
seeing only darkly

through a glass of stout.

Behind the veil

Snow is falling
from a sky of crushed coconut;
traffic crawls,
a few trussed figures struggle by,
their record soon wiped out,
shops are luminous
with things you want to touch.

Evergreens stand like brides
in frilled and sequinned gowns,
a woman from a Thomas Hardy scene
comes toiling up a winding track
but dogs and children
roll together on the ground.

Birds in patchwork raid a plate
and through the glass
my kitten tries to catch the flakes,
then turns to me with saucer eyes.

And now, behind the veil
I am an arrow,
penetrating to the heart of things,
feeling their resonance.

The veil lifted

The snow is melting now
and even evergreens are grey;
traffic tears off
loud with testosterone,
streets and houses
resume dictionary definitions,
named and numbered,
roofs stacked tidy down the bank,
and people scurry to the daily round.

Across the road, machines
locked like panthers on their prey
amputate branches, strip foliage
with crack and splinter,
leaving only sawdust now
round Mr Goldman's limousine.

And once again I feel weary,
living in a world a world away.

The old Black Country

Dirty is a paltry word
for what was there,
if only you could take in
a startling parallel world:

Jungles of plant, machinery
and slag hills piled round factories,
tall chimneys ever smoking,
winding gear wheels ever spinning.

And hammering, cutting, grinding,
thud and shudder,
sudden boom, screech of steam.

Wheels, wheels,
up and down, to and fro,
little trains creeping up hills,
trucks clanking over humpback bridges,
barges, showing up gaudy,
chugging down canals;
all with coal, iron ore, metal
pin to piledriver:
an intrigue of process,
a rhythm in invention.

And *sunsets* - every colour,
gossamer, mottled
in wisps and swirls.

Then at night
silhouette shows,
flashes, sparklers, leaping flame,
liquid white, silver splashes,
turning oily pools
to a shivering rainbow.

Potteries afternoon (1966)

Rain struggles down my window
and houses straggle up the hillsides
through the scrapyard city.

Among the countless tracks like lacerations
a train jerks into life, crawls off
with mounds of china clay,
threading through a fungus crop of chimneys
that gush black smoke, dart flame
(why do you shiver?)
or puff contented, guarding
dumpy kilns which nestle in between.

The train winds on
where children play
defying wasted washing lines
and potholed corridors of brick;
on round heaps of dead and deadening slag
and scratchy grass cringing below
the hoardings calling Marstons Bittermen.

Past monstrous timers
sifting away a hundred thousand lives;
beside the streets
with corner curiosity shops
where men spit
into the litter and the mush
and queue for rock and chips;

where billboards for the local rag
proclaim Bob Hallam, Ace of Clubs
and lights stab out, mid-afternoon,
as a thousand curtains start to slide
across the walls of china ducks.

Killer castle

Battlements which once poured scorn
fouled, torn down, scattered;
on the walls that stand,
shades of ingested emblems,
emblazonry curling like pared skin.

You feel the creeping cold
as an orphan would
and look around, behind.

And through those walls
you see soldiers
hot in gorging, fornicating,
spring up,
fling on helmets, mail;
but still death storms in
and seizes hearts for booty.

Not pain enough!
Their memory too must be vampirized,
their monument bled white.

Escape!
Before this place consumes you,
shaking with silent laughter.

London Pride

London Pride has been handed down to us,
born to rule in this merry old sod;
all the best is in this great town for us,
Nature's law and commandment of God.

London Pride looks down on the rest of us,
yet it swells from the talents we show;
leaves just crumbs thrown down for the best of us,
London Pride is the provinces' woe.

London Pride boasted grace and quality,
now it grafts for the jam and the wealth;
spiel and kitsch ruin all our jollity:
London Pride is consuming itself.

Guest house

Time has died
on London guest house streets
where the eternal monotone
swishes past moulded rows
of yellowed facades
and peeling pseudo-colonnades.

In number 49
faces shrink from touch
behind the curtain shrouds
while grey groups huddle
round the inescapable fried cod.

A glow filters from the back,
a damp-browned sign reads "Vacancies"
and in the yard
bony cats creep round bins
forever overflowing.

From below comes excess clatter
and a song protests its cheer
through the smell of cabbage water.

Garden Suburb

This place keeps hanging on …
no hub, no laid-back rendezvous;
houses, synagogues,
rural cameos apportioned,
a cross section through planners' brains.

All about getting and keeping.

A glut of estate agents,
solicitors and banks;
private patrols, public sirens,
public fears invading private selves.

All about getting and keeping.

Behind the tallest hedges
lie velvet lawns and topiary,
recoiling residences
possessed by grilles, alarms and CTV
and yet in styles which shout:
but the owners pass through like ghosts.

All about getting and keeping.

I want to rush out naked
down this city corridor,
shouting "There's so much *more!*"

Because unless I find the exit soon
inspiration may die.

South from Waterloo

I shrink, squeezed into shadow
by overbearing ranks
that glint, glare down,
elbowing for a patch
and only through chinks
the background city peeps.

Now come business parks,
a waste land of numbered plots,
incontinence of dovetailing,
a jungle of signs and directions.

Further on, a blight
left just roofs to the far horizon,
the River Wandle dribbling through,
a fixation of little square homes
with little square offspring,
crammed tight to keep out curves.

And bridges,
bridges vaulting over bridges,
bearing a tangle of tracks
to the unravelling at Clapham Junction.

Land & Sea

Seascapes

I

Today the sea is object,
ploughed up by prows,
scored by boards and skis,
swept aside by arms and legs.

People saunter
down the Esplanade, absent-smiling.

Young professionals shape the shore:
architects building battlements,
engineers of canals,
marine jewellers.

Players too:
tumbling down dunes,
bouncing gaudy balls about,
digging and dodging with dogs:

the pleasures of parents and children,
and parent-children.

II

But now the sea is renegade,
goaded from deep,
rising, thickening like soup,
throws fits, bores down,
drives up great serpent-waves,
at one with the thunderous sky,

wheeling gulls, screaming wind;
flays the Esplanade,
hurling wood and glass
in clouds of blinding sand.

And people's blood runs cold
with fears they dare not own.

Sky pageant

I

A golden blanket
so rare in its infinite embrace;
and after all my growing
I find myself
reaching out again
to enclose, be enclosed in
a golden blanket.

II

Then a scatter of burning coals,
red heat at the core
tingeing the charcoal edges mauve
on an ashen hearth;
it seems insistent on its nature,
but when I look later
is only embers, raked over.

III

Next, an inflammation
flaring from its sinking core,
searing away all pallor,
and against it
blackened limbs in spasm.

I watch on edge
until a cloud, suspended,
flat-bottomed, Dali-style,
reflects the inferno
chillingly.

November leaves

The plain grey backdrop spotlights
the many sides of leaves:

shaken, bounced, churned
like fairground thrills;

done shimmering in summer,
now slowly glowing embers;

starting out among the evergreens
in every shade from calm to frenzy;

meandering like powdered snow,
drifting down or manic-dancing;

fallen, to cushion raindrops
and gladden the mind;

for burning or digging in
or prized for winter sleep.

Suddenly I feel a chill
and ponder choices dragging on

and new leaves
which must be evergreen.

60s country station

The old train comes bowling in –
brakes with a broken bagpipe din,
pitching me forwards;
then leaning out,
I see boarded rooms,
a dozing engine breathing gently,
little flower beds
lately fringed with shells
which progressive weeds are closing down
and on the platform no feet sound.

At last the stationmaster
in remnants of a uniform
emerges, frees a Test match commentary,
consults his pocket watch
and saunters down
to chinwag with the guard.

Then an oily flag,
a heavy clank, insistent blast,
we lurch forward, pull away,
and looking back
I say a last goodbye.

Soon the rationalised world
is in my face again:
I sigh.

Country station view

I lean out
(can I *really* hear
the faintest crackle in the air?)
and smile again to see this stop
among the cabbages and corn.

A terracotta roof peeps out
cradled by a wood and daisy-bosomed bank,
a plough is rusting in its final furrow,
a bleached track winds over a hill,
leading on to warm imaginings.

Now through a golden cloud
a harvester comes on – and on,
almost to the railway fence
then turns upon its beaten track,
and in the chattering rise and fall
I feel the long slow pulse of summer,
its end and sure return.

Echoes of the mill

I'm leaning over this bridge once more,
distant on a summer day ...

The wheel was always turning
at the old mill house
which thrust out,
though the river didn't need restraint
as it toiled past the brine baths.

There were always swans
coasting by or begging
on the poplar walk,
and echoes of my childhood
in the cries of nursery children.

And a yearning fills me
for when people and summers
seemed to be for ever.

Pictures of Cannock Chase

Twilight on windy Milford hills:
deformed trees like spirits damned
thresh about, fling out arms
which clutch at empty air.
My hand seeks solid hold,
yet further off
fields and forest lie as still
as pages in an atlas.

*   *   *

A clammy afternoon in Sherbrook:
an arbour of khaki light
beneath a tent of greenery;
from pregnant boles
exotic flowers burst,
first your voice, then your mind
is charmed away,
to thoughts of enchanted gardens
of ancient folk lore.

*   *   *

With the dusk comes
the strangest purring sound,

you turn and turn about:
No use; the nightjar is a bird full of twilight.

This place is strange, other-worldly;
you tell yourself you've just been fantasizing ...

But are you *sure?*

Virgin land

So high in dense-wooded hills,
looking down on the toy town,
and now I'm coming through cloud
to a place squeezed by earth and sky:
cider, fruits, clotted cream for sale
and carted round the farms;
people congeal in a pub-cum-everything,
on horseback, greet each other
with seeming brotherhood,
and me with friendly curiosity.

Traces of a time when living
for the bounty and the beauty
bore natural values for fulfilment:
people were partners with the world.

What a discovery!
A virgin land I'd never colonise
but be absorbed, explored in.

Then inspiration drains:
I must start back.
Of course!
The tyrant struggle never yields for long.

Ghosts of the quays

The new Exeter Quays:
trendy shops, arts and crafts,
night life, crowds;
yet clinging to the old quay,
the converted custom house

and the ghosts:
Men eking out a ledge,
digging canals, a basin,
building locks, a weir,
all to beat the silt
and bring the barges in;

figures squeezing through
an alley warren
with crates and bundles,
silent in the dark,
then vanishing;
on unofficial business;

merchants who watch men
hacking earth and rock,
packing wool in arches,
milling, drying.
Some Dutchmen,
in gabled houses
strange among the cottages,

who tally, scrutinize,
fold, stack in place,
nodding slowly.

And then the merchants dine
on venison and claret
amid carved oak and coats of arms;
and looking on the quays today
they smile.

Town v Country

The city comes from Using Man,
his short-term plan, and more's the pity,
there's art – no doubt; but hype, quick sale;
attractions never fail, pleasure's all about,
you're thrilled, impressed: but mind the snare,
don't be a bear all circus-dressed.

The country lets you *be*: with peace and time
you feel the chime with land and sea;
the core shows how and why you're *you*,
and values, ways to balance and endure:
then from the whole, in any place,
you can embrace a wider role.

Creatures

Avian charmers

Tits

They zip in
with flight like whooping cheers,
in soft olive, blue and gold
with tetchy ticking off,
twitch, switch around the feast,
heads blurring in a mist of fat;
then stop: dart glances round
like urchins breaking rules,
and from behind the meal
peep faces, upside down.

Robin

We love the robin,
thinking he loves us:
his puffed-out breast makes *us* glow,
he squats in our property
and almost in our faces
thrills us with exultant song.
He tilts his head, a black eye gleams;
surely this delightful nuisance
seeks our company?

Not so!
He only seeks domain:
we are the usurpers,
and cursing that he cannot drive us out,
he settles for the next best thing.

Wagtails

On the ground, the wagtails move
like clockwork toys
with springs gone wrong;
heads and tails that wobble,
zigzags, gone then back,
mad bursts of speed;
they paddle long in puddles,
sail over humps,
pick out food with brisk gentility.

But by streams they give air shows,
twist, tack or hang
then zoom to snatch their prey
and landing, tilt and fan their tails
with flash of yellow, black and white.

Before, you stood and smiled,
but now you stand ... and stand:
and oddity and grace
oddly no longer contradict
but complement delight.

Starlings

They drop like litter
on town streets
and swagger off,
the Wild Bunch, partners in grime.

But rooftops stage a solo act:
with bristling throat,
neck that cranes and shrinks,
wings trailing like a panto villain's cloak;
a mimic's repertoire
from fascination you can *feel*.

Then at twilight
birds swarm, mass in clouds,
evaporate, re-form,
swirl down like autumn gusts
and up again in twisters:
a Northern Lights in monochrome.

How strange,
this clown-cum-enchanter,
this smutty stand-up comic,
raising sniggers on street corners
yet lifting our hearts to the skies.

Ducks

They splash down on swatter feet
straight into a social hub,
heads together, tails wagging,
with undertones of quacks and chuckles;
upend or dive
all the length of your bated breath
then pop up like corks
to preen and dabble,
celebrate in splashing.

Sometimes they even sail serene
in motley convoys;
then waddle up the bank
like corpulent old folks
to snooze with one eye flickering.

Waders

A living storm cloud breaks
upon the shore,
a winged deluge sounds;
moving in drifts and swells
a thicket of legs twinkles over the sand,
the dumpy host homes in as one.

Then they break up, scurry,
a thousand bills pepper the earth,
comb the pools, sweep, pry, spear.

What joy in their obsessive art!
What virtue in necessity!

Vietcong

The urban pigeons' motto might well be
"Floere et restabit", had they the knowledge;
for they have traded wildness and much toil
for just a mess of porridge.

They brave the traffic, battery of boots
to stay at Hotel Man – and celebrate;
though rooms are rough and food is Cordon Gris
it's always on a plate.

They snatch and gobble every crumb
and even courtship has a crunch;
males pirouette and bow, with rippling croons
but then knock off for lunch.

They lie like dollops on our roofs,
drop down chimneys, scratch away cement;
pretend to nest with feathers, scattered twigs,
dissolve our buildings with their excrement.

So people lash up nets and drive in spikes
to keep them *out*, for heaven's sake;
yet still they cling, squeeze in and see no mess
but just a piece of cake.

At last we poison, set our hawks on them,
but like the Vietcong they come together;
for men may come and men may go
but pigeons live for ever.

Butterflies

Born out of scattered sunlight
they blaze out, glow or blend;

in digressing dances
they savour aerial mysteries;

they spread their glory, inspire
a spreading summer mood;

then autumn comes:
they're gone.

The Reverend Bug

He started from the draining board,
this little beetle on the wall;
up, down; stop, go; to, fro -
and back to start.

Still, on this glossy, endless plain
he perseveres;
and I revere his labour and his gutsiness.

Then I recall he hasn't fed,
I launch him from the window:
See his tiny wings go!

Joybringer

The little dog has doubtful pedigree,
short to the knee, body too long and round
but always a definite black and white;

I take a delight in his lolloping gait,
the sight of him always spurs a smile;
the world is warmer to embrace.

People

Bike boys

A summer evening:
I join the bike boys
mounted, propped against the fence
or hanging round a heap of steel,
a sprawl of noise and colour
with horseplay, gusts of laughter,
tales and easy talk,
all between the swigs of Coke.

Dave's radio plays *Ticket to ride*
while Baz and Johnny thin it down;
Roy, overdue home,
picks specks off his clothes;
Miff's resounding in obscenities;
Tony plans to zoom around the Chase:
What joy!

Now comes the ice cream van;
we suck a scattered rainbow,
Linda and Jen run out
and Dickie drops his pants:
girls shriek, boys roar.

Gradually (Roy first)
they start to drift away
and I'm getting restless:
I want much more than this ...

and yet begrudge their reckless confidence ...
I'm in a no man's land.

I trudge back up the drive,
kicking stones into the hedge:
Why did I never have a bike?

Men of clay

O Sunday soccer men of clay,
let me tell your story:

You have no stars, no history,
no medals, boardroom silverware,
to give that climbing glow,
sense of embrace;
just Smith and Jones and now
is all *you* get.

You have no home,
no state of art arena
humming with resources;
just a bumpy patch,
hired brick huts
where showers are a lottery,
hands heave on chains,
with the compounded smell
of toilets, damp,
and the unfailing embrocation remedy.

You have no following:
your entrance brings no roar
throbbing from tiers that shrink the sky;
just a few cheers
from mates, loose-enders
and the man with the magic sponge.

You have no record,
no TV cameras, DVDs,
no breathless pressman snatching up the phone;
just verbal replays,
memories which drain
with every glass.

So what's the point?
Why the grunts, calls, curses,
flesh striving after intention?

Because you're moved by visions,
your minds are full of dreams.

Breadless in Battersea

Door wrenched open,
Motown unleashed,
his voice pinched in mimicry,
heavy soles stomping down.

Just a smile opens my door,
he deflates onto the bed,
gulps my coffee
and behind a cloud of smoke
a grin spreads,
sly and slow.

And then he makes his pitch:
"That bastard Jamie promised me a job,
let me down again -
after all I done for him!
Now the dole is tightening up;
must do Ernie's meter
and as for rent – No way!

Wish I could get some bread together!

Met this chick:
bottle blonde, big tits,
could've boogied
till the cows come home;
said I'd take her out
but I dunno

Got no bread just now ...

God! Ya should've seen
this motor down the road:
stereo, recliners – *the lot!*
bit like one I used to have ...
Yeah, right – forget it!
Know my trouble, man?

I never got no bread."

He looks at me and sighs,
drags himself up,
stubs another fag out in the sink,
and cursing, kicks his whining cat
and sets off down his Nan's for lunch.

And I tidy up ferociously
till something in his sail-on soul,
his living from the gut,
resonates; a smile breaks out,
I want to rush out like a child
and roll on new-sprung green.

Small-town

The place has posters for exotic destinations,
West End shows,
and a sticker for coach tickets.

The young man
has a designer hairstyle
and a Surreyfied Cockney accent.

"A return to Llanelli, please."
　"Where's *that?*"
"South Wales."
　"Has civilisation *reached* yet?"
"I know there are coaches!"
　"How are you spelling it?"...
(flicks through a guide; laughs):
　"Yeah, Fridays only:
'spect they all come out and stare!"
"Oh, all right! I'll go to Swansea
and get a train."
　"Yeah – or a donkey!"

I take my ticket and go.
It wasn't worth hitting him:
I'd never have broken the skin.

L.A. girls

I wish they all were L.A. girls!
I dither over style and hue
as Debs rolls out the seventh blue
and smiling Jill says "Try the swirls."

How could I be so green, perverse,
to wish they all were L.A. girls?
'cos now my fantasy unfurls:
they're only charming from my purse!

But *no!* They hadn't tossed their curls
to make a sale, but worked to suit –
and surely that comes from the root;
the setting just shows off the pearls:

Hooray for Laura Ashley girls!

Hospital days

I

Questions, questions,
tests, scans, measurements,
orders: "Drink water, pass urine";
notes, charts, assessments:

but no answers.

Cleaners, sheet changers,
shop trolley, tea ladies,
more water (more urine)

but no answers.

Doctors, consultants,
students packing round,
more questions,
a few results and explanations

but no answers.

Nurses: some feelers,
with feelers for their work;
others dawdle, chatter, forget,
have favourites:

but no answers.

Staff peering at screens:
histories, on-line diagnosis,
data equals treatment,

but *still* no answers.

Then the procedure:
blood, soreness, burning;
details and instructions:

And finally some answers.

II

A slow afternoon ...
sunk in my cubicle
I take in once more
the code of practice on the wall,
gentle rumble of the ventilator,
someone idly turning a page.

So much, *too* much time
to ponder on my life ...

Down the corridor,
wheels, directed footsteps,
snatches of chat and laughter,
common goals, easy company.

All like time, passing,
passing me by.

III

Lost in thinking
and not thinking:
not in the mood for the others ...

But just a look, a smile,
and I'm breaking out;
we talk about our ailments:

the Bangladeshi breaks my heart
with his trials
in claiming a rent-free flat.

I relish football chat
with the Blackburn Rovers fan,
admire his sweet and caring wife
who visits every day.

Linda from Clinical Trials
brings a paper she bought herself,
walks me down the corridors,
connects me to my strength again.

And I want to keep in focus
the human kind in others
which brings out mine.

IV

From the corner of the ward
that's fading from him
Charlie struggles up,
cries out in dread as much as pain,
can't make it -
gushes blood and shit.

A cleaner drags a filthy mop across,
mutters "Filthy man!":
I could choke her.

My feelings rush to him
like a mother,
but meet the real man;
my tongue is stuck or speaks platitudes:
he'll despise me
and I can't stand that.

I feel like clutter,
soon find myself avoiding him.
My heart had seemed full
of empathy and care

but my heart lied.

Leaving hospital

Out in a blur
to a rainy afternoon:
the city's self-righteous stir
hits me like a gale,
pairing relief with fears
of another alien stretch.

But in the back seat
I wrap up in a rug;
streets and buildings
are still coming-to,
shapes loom out of the spray,
rumble, sharpen, melt again.

A woman with an Alsatian
in a sudden emerald park
is zooming in; my hands
had started defending.

The ivy-clad Warwick Castle feels welcoming;
lights blaze out,
and was that a party I saw inside?

Then the driver speaks ...
familiar sights,
and I am more and less alive.

The other side

He always appears at lunchtime,
wearing the coat he always wore
and wanders towards the greasy caff.

You approach him in the street,
he melts over to the other side;
his doormat reads "Go away."

Stopping dead, he stares
at people living daily lives:
Is he astonished? Contemptuous?
Or longing to take part?

Nemesis

On a train in mid-morning
come father and daughter
and squeeze in beside me;
he sits her on his knee
and she, nursing yet needing,
embraces him with lingering care,
but only for the man beneath the skin.

They sight landmarks,
make up games,
laugh and chatter,
cocooned, with enchanted eyes.

Now memories of all my years
deep-vaulted, inflated,
cheating on returns,
come hunting me down again.

And once more I'm sinking:
will I always be alone,
at times a friend of fathers,
but never father loved as friend?

Coach company

Heathrow –
and you hear them coming ...
Ma first:
huge straw hat,
boxes, parcels, carrier bags,
baby slung at the breast,
bumps and jolts and bulges.

Then the kids:
baseball caps, games,
chewing, then suddenly quiet.

Last comes Dad:
Stetson and shorts,
enormous backpack
and headphone salvation.

Ma organises:
"You two together ...
No – sit *there!*"

They cram the stuff
onto racks, under seats,
but it still falls out;
someone needs to reach the toilet –
"Ooh, *sorry!*"

The baby is grizzling,
Ma rocks it heavily;
it grizzles on.

The kids were straight
into their laptops,
feeding themselves crisps, chocolate,
without moving their heads.

Ma is expanding to someone:
"Yes, Disneyworld;
Ooh, *lovely* hotel
and the kids *loved* it!"

My inside is knotted
but its O.K. for Dad:
he's got his anaesthetic.

Bach-ing mad

Johann Sebastian Bach is your man
if you're after a good mechanic,
with a pop-a-pa pop-a-pa pop for a plan
Johann Sebastian Bach is your man,
religiously saying all that he can;
and it's all such a scream, so very Germanic,

Johann Sebastian Bach is your man –
if you're after a good mechanic.

Ode to Sibelius

Your critics are echoing again:
"Mere nationalism!", "Nature stuff!"

How could *that* galvanize my inner life?

But your growling chords,
the warring clap and tear
raise conflicts, inside and out,
want, despair
and something louring, poised;
I clench and quiver.

Then a flitting, even playful step,
rays burst through,
are lost, found again,
merge into beams;
blood surges, spirit swells
and with a blare of brass
the radiant light sweeps out;
I feel my further self, stand dumb.

Till finally, in quietly musing strings
I sense myself
in the still, silent panorama
and the ground of both,
with hope of flawed fruition,
a noble, melancholy balancing.

This is *Man's* nature in Nature,
not revealed by construct, rules,
fashion of time or place,
but only by sharing of the heartbeat
in forms like nutshells of the universe.

And can your critics,
from *their* place,
even imagine such an art?

The harpist

She starts with feather touch
which lingers in places
prompting whispers and sighs;
then a massage, strings quivering,
hands sweep over, fingers fly,
stroking deeper;
she throws herself in,
undulating to crescendo
then sinks back,
the last note held and hushed.

Sailors and others

I

Nautical objects surround us
and at the bar there's a man
in navy blazer, slacks,
sipping wine:
"Came down here for the boat ...
Well, I know a bit;
computer does the rest ...
Off to Bermuda on Friday."

I turn to a leathery fisherman,
cable-knitted,
draining the local brew:
"Yeah, eschawry can be tricky,
but yaw knauw tha banks and toides;
yaw witch tha wind and waves;
yaw get tha *feel* ...
Yeah, oi bin fishin' 'ere
Orl moi loife."

II

All around are old photos
of lifeboats, crews,
the folk they saved and lost;
you feel the joy
of grasping solid ground
and the uprush
of epidemic mourning.

But how can a lubber understand
lives willed to the waves
for utter strangers?
A lust for glory?
Some heightened fellow-feeling?
A thrill to fight the sea?

Or just gut-sensing the destiny
of elements to menace Man;
of Man, to try and tame them?

Soul of Sidmouth

Henry has retired now;
he sallies out
from his Regency residence
and starts his routine:

walk for the Labrador
in the landscaped floral gardens,
bowls which roll on glassy lawns,
lunch with friends
at the Conservative Club,
watch a bit of cricket.

With Amy, first to Fields
for her new silk scarf,
then coffee, or maybe cream tea
in the Old Town,
all cobbles, alleys
and fishermen's cottages;

an evening stroll
along the Esplanade,
still reminiscent of
horse-drawn carriages
and elevated patronage;
perhaps a Pavilion show
if there's something decent on.

Hush, you screeching socialists!
and thank the Henrys
and this place;
at least, for keeping values
like beauty, peace and permanence.